The Shape of the World

Triangles

Dana Meachen Rau

Marshall Cavendish
Benchmark
New York

Triangles are tall.

3

Triangles are tools.

5

Triangles are fun.

Triangles are messy.

Triangles bite.

Triangles grow.

13

Triangles make music.

15

Triangles say go slow.

17

You can make a triangle!

19

Triangles

mountain

pizza

rake

sign

swing set

teeth

trees

triangle

Index

Page numbers in **boldface** are illustrations.

About the Author

Dana Meachen Rau is an author, editor, and illustrator. A graduate of Trinity College in Hartford, Connecticut, she has written more than one hundred fifty books for children, including nonfiction, biographies, early readers, and historical fiction. She lives with her family in Burlington, Connecticut.

Reading Consultants

Nanci Vargus, Ed.D. is an Assistant Professor of Elementary Education at the University of Indianapolis.

Beth Walker Gambro received her M.S. Ed. Reading from the University of St. Francis, Joliet, Illinois.

With thanks to Nanci Vargus, Ed.D. and
Beth Walker Gambro, reading consultants

Marshall Cavendish Benchmark
Marshall Cavendish
99 White Plains Road
Tarrytown, New York 10591-9001
www.marshallcavendish.us

Library of Congress Cataloging-in-Publication Data

Rau, Dana Meachen, 1971–
Triangles / by Dana Meachen Rau.
p. cm. — (Bookworms. The shape of the world)
Summary: "Identifies triangles in the world"—Provided by publisher.
Includes index.
ISBN-13: 978-0-7614-2286-0
ISBN-10: 0-7614-2286-2
1. Triangle—Juvenile literature. 2. Geometry, Plane—Juvenile literature.
I. Title. II. Series.
QA482.R286 2006
516'.154—dc22
2005032459

Photo Research by Anne Burns Images

Cover Photos by Corbis/Royalty Free and Corbis/Matthias Kulka/zefa

The photographs in this book are used with permission and through the courtesy of:
Corbis: pp. 1, 13, 21bl Craig Tuttle; pp. 7, 21tl Jennie Woodcock/Reflections Photolibrary; pp. 11, 21tr Tim Davis;
pp. 15, 21br Norbert Schaefer; p. 19 Tom & Dee Ann McCarthy. Getty Images: pp. 3, 9, 20tl, 20tr.
SuperStock: pp. 5, 20bl Comstock; pp. 17, 20br age fotostock.

Printed in Malaysia
1 3 5 6 4 2